FOURTH ORGANON

Advanced and applied mysticism For Twenty first century!

SHAH RAM

Copyright © 2019 Shah Ram.

All rights reserved. No part of this book may be used or reproduced by any means, graphic, electronic, or mechanical, including photocopying, recording, taping or by any information storage retrieval system without the written permission of the author except in the case of brief quotations embodied in critical articles and reviews.

Balboa Press books may be ordered through booksellers or by contacting:

Balboa Press
A Division of Hay House
1663 Liberty Drive
Bloomington, IN 47403
www.balboapress.com
1 (877) 407-4847

Because of the dynamic nature of the Internet, any web addresses or links contained in this book may have changed since publication and may no longer be valid. The views expressed in this work are solely those of the author and do not necessarily reflect the views of the publisher, and the publisher hereby disclaims any responsibility for them.

The author of this book does not dispense medical advice or prescribe the use of any technique as a form of treatment for physical, emotional, or medical problems without the advice of a physician, either directly or indirectly. The intent of the author is only to offer information of a general nature to help you in your quest for emotional and spiritual well-being. In the event you use any of the information in this book for yourself, which is your constitutional right, the author and the publisher assume no responsibility for your actions.

Any people depicted in stock imagery provided by Getty Images are models, and such images are being used for illustrative purposes only.
Certain stock imagery © Getty Images.

Print information available on the last page.

ISBN: 978-1-9822-2798-2 (sc)
ISBN: 978-1-9822-2894-1 (hc)
ISBN: 978-1-9822-2799-9 (e)

Library of Congress Control Number: 2019906940

Balboa Press rev. date: 05/31/2019

FOURTH ORGANON

CONTENTS

Master's letter ix
Writer's preface xiii
What do we want!? xvii

SELF-REALIZATION
Introduction to the first section 1
There is no short-cut! 3
Devil versus God. Consciousness is multi-layered 5
How human being is created? 9
Show must goes on! 15
I know that I know 19
Basics of spiritual paths 21
The theorem of Karma and retribution for action 25
Reincarnation; Does it happens always? 29
Dreams and lucid dreaming 35
Astrology and horoscope 39
Laws of numbers and the law of octaves 43
Male-female relationship 45
Purpose of creation 49
What do old religions say? 53
Authority and power versus humility 55
Kundalini a way to power!? 59
Man of God (MOG) 61
Psychedelic drugs 65
Exercises for reaching self-realization 67

GOD-REALIZATION
Preface 77
What is God-Realization...79
Final advises and Master's last 81

MASTER'S LETTER

In last few 300 years and after the era of enlightenment, great progresses happened in human being's position in universe. But there is no answer for after death states and supernatural matters in the books of this period. Every human being has a strange attraction to these matters and that is why, after ~300 years and at the beginnings of the 21th century deceptive religious men and semiconscious extremists are coming to the game to save the people and guarantee them a good after death life!!

There existed an old belief that the pure knowledge to supernatural matters should be kept hidden from social and average people, and instead some nonsense about heaven and hell should be deduced to people's mind. In this belief, religious men (though some of them knew the real story) distributed wrong concepts about god and undetectable parts of universe. This wrong idea, though were useful for few years, now, not only are useless but also are harmful and dangerous.

Now in 21th century, it seems that the only way to stop the complicated and turbulent extremists from burning the earth is to spread the pure and real knowledge of mythology about god and human. Though some rare rash humans may even misuse this knowledge, but when everybody has the real knowledge, these creatures can be stopped easily or would not be able to gather innocent people around themselves.

A few decades after birth, and searching for common aims like earning money, finding good jobs, and a beautiful or handsome lover, making happy family, and etc, many of human beings with at least an average level of intelligence, start to ask questions like; who really am I?, what happens to me after death?, why peoples with bad minds and dark activities are also happy and successful!? ….

Reading religious books to find the answer to these questions is useless, at least in this high level of social knowledge. On the other hand in 20th century many sophistic and mystic groups (mostly with an Indian origin) tried to give some vague answers to these questions but involuntarily, or may be purposefully didn't mention the real story.

I believe that; the real knowledge to these should be accessible to all and protection of them from mercenary men should be done by higher levels of consciousness. It seems to me that no human being is in the position to decide that, this knowledge should be given to Mr. A and should not be given Mr. or Mrs. B.

In the path of mysticism or theosophy or what else one may call it the first aim is to reach self-realization, and after that, for shaking out final doubts and find the real reason of your path, one should try to experience god-realization. See carefully what I say:

- Always do the exercises of self-realization meaningful mindful and purposeful. Never mimic others(who may even call themselves master) blind folded. It is best to invent new exercises for yourself and use ancient exercises simply as a guide. The era of master- disciple relation is ended you should become a real master.
- Never become satisfied with your spiritual progresses. Move ahead, and never get satisfied of experiencing some supernatural events which are routine when you begin the path.
- After a few years of staying in the path of mysticism you will become the king of your world. Everything will lay under your

control and life become very beautiful. Don't even then stop! This is not what you were searching for. Move ahead!
- Though no one will find the ultimate reality (since it is not fixed and always changes because of highly multi-dimensionality) but the important thing is to Walk Toward It.

Finally I should mention a word with politicians:" we are at the beginning years of the Aquarius epoch. This era which will last a millennium is, and should be, the era of peace and knowledge. So, it is very important for –at least talent-politicians and economists, to let, a new and peaceful arrangement of human being in this planet happens".

This book is prepared by one of my, moderate, students, to ensure you that there is no life after death if you fail in creating a body not in need of food and water. So, if you don't want to die like a miserable animal, do the practices carefully and sacrifice your time as much as possible for this aim.

WRITER'S PREFACE

After a long history of mysticism and theosophy and gathering of a huge amount of precious knowledge about human's and ultra-human super-consciousness, it seems that the best way to answer all the metaphysical questions – that occur in the mind of everyone with a sufficient amount of curiosity about the universe- is; to experience a "non-body dependent, separate consciousness" directly.

Most of us (as science based beings) are pushed to believe that ; our consciousness is a consequence of our brain activity and when we die, cause of destruction of our brain cells, nothing would be left.

On the other hand, all religions and some philosophers believe in some kind of after death existence, which is not well defined and is non-rational. Like this: "there are places in other world in which, peoples are burning all around the clock" or some other amusing descriptions about heaven. The best way to solve the problem, and giving an exact answer to endless demands of human being for after death life, is to teach every interested person to experience "non- body dependent consciousness".

In last few centuries and especially 20th century, hundreds of Middle Eastern, Indian, Chinese, Persian and American theosophists claimed that they can guide their followers to self- and god realization. But though many of them were of some use and each added a color to the great picture of mysticism on earth, we should know that the whole painting is different from each color alone.

In this book, at the same time that we mention the existing total knowledge of mysticism- that are gathered from Persian, Tibetan, Indian, Mexican and Jewish ancient books- add the final color or real story to it.

Some may criticize us that; this knowledge should be kept private from general population. We should remind them that; those people who find the prophecy of this book will never misuse it and those rear people with semi-dark mind that may find enough forbearance to read this book would be much easier to be stopped since the reality is disseminated in public.

So, let's begin by mentioning some prerequisites!

1st- It is better to put aside a part of everyday life as "out of earth hobbies "for your contemplations and exercises.

2nd- Make yourself prepared for a period of at least 10-15 years of study and practice, to reach non-body dependent consciousness or self-realization, though rarely some may reach it faster.

3rd- Before starting this book, begin this recitation that is taken from Toussbaba website: "O… God, the great consciousness of the cosmos; keep my consciousness immune from superstitious beliefs and religious fanaticism". You should repeat this on night time before sleep, and on morning immediately after awakening, for ~ two weeks.

4th- Try to find the following books and read them successively in the 10 years that you have ahead! They are written by good people in love to help humanity. And, try to read again- or at least take a look at- this book every year.

1- Star signs by: Linda Goodman
2- Third eye by: Rampa
3- Be here now by: Ram Dass (1971)
4- Meditation; The art of inner ecstasy by: Osho

5- The Tiger's fang by: Paul Twitchell(1967)
6- The key to secret world by: p. Twitchell (1969)
7- Journey to Ixtalan by: Carlos Castanda
8- Art of dreaming by: Carlos Castanda
9- Dream yoga By: Chogyal Nakai Norbu and Micheal Katz
10- Heart drops of dharmakaya By: Shardza Tashi Gyaltsen
11- Tertium organon by: P.D. Ouspensky (1922)
12- Zhi-Khro By: Khenchen Palden Sherab translated by: Khenpo Tse Wang Dogyal
13- The flight of Garuda by: Padmasambhava, Shabkar Tsugdruk Rangdra Translated by: Keith Dowman(1994)
14- The circuit of force by: Dion fortune, Gareth Knight (1998)
15- Hekmat-al-eshragh by: S. Sohrevardi
16- With you until eternity by: Rampa
17- The Psychedelic experience by: Timothy Leary, Ralph metzner, Richard Alpert
18- Transcendental magic By: Eliphas Levi
19- Active side of infinity by: Carlos Castanda
20- In search of the miraculous by: P. D. Ouspensky
21- The Shariyat-Ki-Sugmad, book 1 and 2, from Eckankar series by: Paul Twitchell
22- Tibetan yoga and secret doctrines second edition (edited) By: W. Y. Evans-Wentz
23- Beelzebub's tale to his grandson by: G.I. Gurdjieff
24- The emerald tablets of Thoth brought to public by:
25- Mesmerism and hypnotism…. Find a suitable book that matches with your mind
26- Life is real only then when I Am By: G.I. Gurdjieff

At the beginning of preparing this book, we were not very interested to continue cause of master's disagreement. But, when I remembered my long years of reading useless books and following false masters, I thought, maybe by preparing this book, won't let this happen to others. And, attracted master's agreement.

Now…, after the "first organon" of Aristotle and the "second organon" of Francis bacon and "third organon" of Ouspensky, it is time for the fourth organon.

With divine love
Sh.Mz.

WHAT DO WE WANT!?

Every human being has a strange attraction toward supernatural matters and God. Why in severe troubles we automatically think about such a super strong thing? When we die does everything ends? Are all of the religious scripts are nonsense and for cheating of the mass, or the base of them are real?

To answer all these questions and many other, and to change life on earth planet from an aimless machinery one to a useful, celestial and energetic one, we should pass two phases. First, reaching a state called Self-realization, which means to find, feel and internalize, what we really are, and what is left of us after death.

Second, reaching God-realization that means, to find deeply what God is and what is going on when we are out of our capsule.

In all of the ancient books and sects of spiritualism, Sufism, Monism, Buddhism and other mysticism, in all of these long years of human history it was insisted that this earthy creation is defective and poisonous and somewhere else or in some other dimensions a very perfect state of creation exists. Rumi said: "This world is a prison and we are the prisoner, dig the wall and free yourself my disciple"!

But now after all this long way we, as spiritual men of the 21th century who possess all the knowledge of the ancient life, proclaim that: This Terrestrial creation is the Best or at least, one of the best option of creation!

So…, what is the purpose of mysticism?

The only point here is that; we believe, this creation can be much better and human beings have much more potentialities than this. They can reach to levels to see the future and live without distractions, fears, hate or anger since they would be able to communicate and ask everything by telepathy, project their love to their lover without fear of rejection, taste a rare delicious fruit in far over the ocean by astral projection, live without the fear of death and so on. We are trying to prepare the situation for existence of super- human beings (in next 200 years) that naturally are clairvoyant.

By following the comments that are mentioned in this book, and by taking a look at the reference books, and of course by doing the exercises with deep understanding, you will find the path, and by staying on it will become a man of God(MOG) before you reach death bardo.

We have found that the life time for contemporary human beings is not enough to reach him/her a sufficient knowledge to let him live happy in earthy life and further prepare him a reliable after death life (which in most of the cases do not exists at all). Every human being when enters to this world is kept for 6 years in home then is released to receive a huge mass of wrong educations from schools and other people, and before finding the outcomes of self-love and lack of conscience, gets old and dies. We have found that in contrary to some ancient beliefs, Reincarnation Don't happens Frequently nowadays. Everybody dies and his consciousness and memory package dissolves in universal or collective consciousness. Or, at best, only a few amount of memories is transferred to next life. In this book we try to familiarize you with advanced mysticism and teach how one can increase the probability of full and conscious (real) reincarnation.

Universe is made of three things: mater, energy and consciousness. Though mater is a compacted pocket of energy, consciousness or knowledge is not a diluted mater or a high vibration of energy. It Is Something Quite Different. Ponder on this and don't forget it.

In the path to higher state/s of consciousness which some call spiritualism some call it Gnosis and we call Mysticism, there are two branches that a seeker should become expert in:

1- Theoretical knowledge
2- Practical mysticism

In the first, your intellectual part/s will be uploaded with knowledge that had been discovered by previous masters up to know (since you shouldn't – and don't have time to - invent the wheel form its beginning!). These knowledge has different names like Tantra, Alchemy, Kabala, Dezogchen, 4th way and etc. A seeker(Rahro) should have at least a thourogh knowledge of all of these from Japanese and Chinese to Indian, Persian, Egyptian, American and Mexican mystic arts (the books in preface will help you to find the best contexts).

The 2nd branch consists of all the exercises that a seeker should do practically during the path. Here lies a very, very, important point!

Every human being (as will be mentioned later) has at least 3 bodies(the whole collection of similar experiences are called" Body"): Physical, emotional, and mental. See me carefully what I say!... About 99.999 % of human forms don't have walled of and well defined emotional and mental bodies. They have something, but it is vague and labile, and never will survive/stay after death. There will be no soul for them after death and if, only for few days. Most of the previous masters are from 0.001% of people whom had those bodies formed- accidentally or through their last period of living. But…, what about you as the seeker/rahro?

You should learn to Create it, meanwhile that you are doing the first theoretical part.

And This is The Very First thing that you should do, to understand what we are talking about. THIS is the only way that you can see and understand what masters said and say: Creation Of A second Body.

Taking a superficial look at the contents of this book might be dangerous and create severe misunderstandings. So, keep your book in a safe place or locker and only borrow it to those who will read the whole book with patience.

SELF-REALIZATION

INTRODUCTION TO THE FIRST SECTION

What are the benefits of reaching self-realization? The main reason is to become the king of your world(not others, yours!). In the beautiful earthy life, it is full of unpredictable unhappy problems that bitter the taste of your experience on this plant. For taking the control of your life in your hand and picking it away from the matter of accidents—that makes tension and stress on you—and become a king,… self-realization is necessary. Only then you can stop many of these bad effects or by predicting them, decrease your tension.

Second; when reaching self-realization, you will be able to keep yourself healthy and experience a life without stress and full of love.

Third; as will be explained later, our universe is laden with consciousness threads or globes. When a special amount of these consciousness globes are packed together like a rosary, (just like a pot keeping a special amount of air molecules) a strange creature named human being is made. When death happens the rosary is torn or by other means the pot breaks, and the consciousness globes become scattered in the universe.

By other means, they become unified with the God (As will be mentioned later reincarnation that is quite true, does not happens always). By reaching self-realization we learn how to preserve our rosary and keep our consciousness after death and destruction of our body. Actually we should learn to create a 2nd and…, 3rd bodies. To create it the best way is by being "Present". Imagine that you are watching yourself from above or back as long as you can. Search in the ref. books we wrote for all the practices referring them.

Meanwhile as we will talk later, you should create a dream body also. For it, teachings about "out of body experience" are helpful that will be mentioned in related chapter.

In current section you will become familiar with the mass knowledge of mysticism which have been gathered in last thousands years of human civilization. Although some part of this puzzle is from Tibet, the other from Persia, and south America or other places, they complete each other strangely. Meanwhile a final solution would be added to the text in it's appropriate time to create a dedication for the human race on the very beginning of the "millennium of peace and love" which should start between years of 2012 to 2035 A.C.

Meanwhile don't forget that we are in one of the best state of creation and your body is like a very unique temple or vehicle which is necessary for reaching God-realization. So take continuous caring of your body. Do regular sport exercises or yoga practices to keep your body healthy and decreasing the velocity of aging process.

THERE IS NO SHORT-CUT!

In the path to self-realization, a seeker/rahro should pass some periods of celibacy, fasting, silence, no meat diet and…. But you should know that when this works right that the student reaches a point that actually he/she don't feel any temptation toward these things. The reverse is not true.

Many followers of most ancient religions and mystic paths had seen that their leaders are not very interested in sexual relation, polyphagia, meat and so on. So they thought that if they go backward and halt these body desires they will reach salvation! A seeker or student can never stop eating meat until he/ she has not experienced it enough. One can never make his/her mind free of thinking about opposite sex if has not experienced it enough time.

But,… how may a seeker/rahro keep himself away from extravagance? The best way is remembrance. This would be discussed later, but means that a student of the path should become able to remember himself in every activity.

The universe is full of consciousness globes or strings. When a defined amount of them are gathered or packed around, an aggregation of knowledge is created. In the earth there is a capacity for this aggregation that, material can gathers around it. Depending on the type and data base of these globes different creatures, and the most interesting of them human being is formed. We have interesting abilities created by our 5 sense organs and being in the path to self-realization do not mean to forget them. In some mystic paths of India, Tibet and middle east the followers torture themselves by severe fasting and long term solitude. These should not be overdosed.

A seeker should know that daily life struggles and activities are very helpful and even necessary for spiritual progress, if he learn not to indulge and dissolve in them. He/she should see the social interacts from out-of-his body, keep away from too much internal talks around them, never complain of his state and never think that he deserves more (self-pity).

DEVIL VERSUS GOD. CONSCIOUSNESS IS MULTI-LAYERED

The next very important thing that should not be underestimated is the Multi-layered pattern of consciousness. Duringd long years of human history, there lived many people, kings and even religious leaders on earth whom believed, and assert that are in connection with God and angles. And; because of that, what they are doing is right! But, when you read their comments and study their activities, will see that they where full of faults and misunderstandings. How is this possible? Alexandra, Chengiz khan, Hitler, and, leaders of most religious extremists believed and believe that they are receiving commands from some unseen higher powers!

As a matter of fact some of them were connected with something but what was wrong? See me carfully what I say:

Body-less consciousness have multiple and multiple layers something like an onion. Each layer is separated from the other with a fine curtain and each level or layer is foolish and unconscious relative to the higher one and that higher one is unconscious and defective relative to the next higher....

Here is the important point hidden. Every level of consciousness sees the lower one as evil, unconscious and dark, and tries to condemn it. But that lower level meanwhile looks at the higher one as light and illuminant and God. So there is no perfect Devil and a devil relative to its higher state may look mighty relative to its lower level.

Now at the beginning of this book it should be emphasized and severely recommended that:

By starting spiritual paths, someday you will be connected(channeled) to other states of consciousness. First; don't become dramatized and satisfied with the very first state of consciousness. Always continue in working on yourself to become connected to the highest state of consciousness possible for you.

Second; you might be connected to lower states. The hall mark of them is insistence on selfishness and the famous phrase of: "I am the only correct path!" LOVE is your only compass that guides you to pole. Any received impulse/s in meditation that guides you far from loving others and respecting other religions is from lower states and should be ignored.

Third: Don't forget that, almost all, of the supernatural and contemplative receptions and prophecies which human had received during all of his civilization- as a whole- and yours as a little part of them are from higher or lower levels of consciousness layers. And almost none of them are from God. On contrary to public belief God in its real meaning is something very unique that though is everywhere and though everything is made of/by it, IS far to connect with.

Anyhow, imagine Mr. Kh. When young or middle aged he feels interested in spiritualism. And, starts to read related books and doing practices. After 6-12 months he starts to have some out of body experiences in sleep and receives divination or consultative comments on his deep meditation and contemplations. He jumps up from his solitude and starts to write books, and wiseacre. And if reach or be interested in governmental power, gives radical orders to "save"! humanity, the way had been advised by his internal voice. See me! Don't fall in these traps.

You as the seeker will meet successive layers of consciousness. Specially the first layers that you might meet, though might be higher than you are ignorant relative to a level higher then itself. So,… be patient and don't become over-impressed.

As the final point, we talked that higher states of consciousness – relative to you- see you as dark ignorant guys. Meanwhile you see them as God or Angels. Now…, ponder on this question! how can you attract their benevolence?

HOW HUMAN BEING IS CREATED?

Before entering this discussion it should be known that an omnipresent "thing" with very higher numbers of dimensions exists everywhere(you will feel and find it after 10-15 years of doing your trainings and exercises). At a very small part of this "thing" and on a small numbers of its dimensions some short living pictures appears which their consequence is appearance of creatures. Ancient Mexican gnostics described this in an interesting language. They said: Universe is made of consciousness in the form of threads or globes. When an especial number and type of these globes are packed together a living organism in 3D space appears, and 4th dimension appears to it as motion.

Anyhow, when this –temporary picture (or as some say thought) appears in that thing-God- its terrestrial counter part is created automatically and instantly with a little phase delay to positivity or negativity. Exactly, this phase difference that occurs because of dimensional difference, determines that the creature becomes male or female. For keeping the balance, the original picture should accept the opposite charge. As a consequence, when you are male your counter-part in God's consciousness becomes female. Let's describe it more and in other language.

See me carfully! We have a non materialistic thing or pure knowledge(Holy Ghost) in one side, In other side there is a compacted materialistic thing(son). To have a connection between these two and for bilateral transfer of data between these two, there exists something that some call it Father or Minor ghost.

That omnipresent knowledge is called "spirit" that very small part or short lived picture which is related to you is called "soul" and you are called "physical body +mind". Pay attention; up to here there is no ether body. We'll turn back to this later but now, don't forget that creation from up to down(from soul to physical body) is immediate and direct but in counter direction, from below to above, needs a mediator that is called Soul body and "real I". This body is, what you should build during your spiritual path. Contrary to old routine belief, Soul body is not something that everybody has and experience the after death life with it!

This picture of us which is with us all life long and has opposite polarity with us, is our agent in other invisible states of consciousness, and the reason that we are always in search of our lost half or partner seems to be this!

The difference between human and most of the other creatures is that in other creatures a duplication never occurs. It means that after the appearance of their picture in god's consciousness they appears(are created) directly. If they meet their opposite sex every year it is only for their programming. This results in the unique ability of us: we know that we know.

Yes! Existence of the thing some call "Father" causes the state that: "we know that we are existing".

(A part of) This body-less copy of us is called "green tara" in Tibetan and Indian mysticism or theosophy, "Taba-tam" in Persian theosophy and "soul" in modern spiritual path.

These mean that, each human is like a super-computer (physical or planetary body) inside another super- super-super-high dimensional computer (Soul or spiritual body).

Human being has been granted another unique option that is specialized for higher dimensional creature. It is the ability and potential to build a mediator between the terrestrial copy and sovereignty picture. This mediator, that is called Ether body or as Gurdjieff named Kesdjon body, fixes your connection and enables you to be in constant conscious relation with God. Many believe that everybody have this ether body but as a matter of fact, in almost all cases, when you don't define and "make" it with your spiritual exercises, it is so fade and wan that can be regarded as nothing.

Now, another question! If we were the "thing" or creator or God or any other name, what would we do to keep this system run? As the first act we should keep one of the computers ignorant about existence of the others. Then, for guarding this, at least two programs should be put in the hard ware of the ignorant computer. The first program; gives you encouragements for some works that you describe as good, and the 2nd program; gives punishments for some other works you have defined as bad works(in this small book there is no space for more detailed descriptions). Only we should answer this question; What for are all of these?

- For creating the energy that keeps the universe on or more definitely for transposing the energy to next level.

This should be reminded; we do not mean that bad acts and good acts are the same. As will be mentioned later, the reason that we prescribe the seekers for doing something we may call it good, is not for consent and satisfaction of the 2nd super-computer or even god(as is in normal people). It is only for reducing the interactions with other souls and persons and to show that you are a good program(to attract the benevolence). Since these interactions and bounds are the worst barrier for spiritual progress. As a matter of fact we, as computers, are connected with each other through that multi dimensional -super -super computer. That is why in your well progressed stages you will see that you can feel others emotions easily.

Back to our discussion; in this way, the first(ignorant) super-computer is always busy by gathering good and bad "karmas" which will let enough exchange of energies for keeping the system on.

To have an exact understanding about Green-tara or Taba-tam or father or minor ghost, is very important in spiritual path to self-realization. See! you should realize yourself from your taba-tam's view, and later for god-realization you should crystallize or unite with Taba-tam. Some masters described 4 bodies for each person; physical, astral or etheric, mind body (that should become the soul) and spirit. For reducing complexity, you can take the taba-tam as another name for the mind body but in a special state. For getting more familiar with taba-tam, see what happens when we want to remember, for example, the name of our teacher of the first grade of our school. First we say that it should be impossible to find it but after a deep pondering our green tara will find it for us(the capacity of our brain is not enough for preserving all of these old memories). At this time, not only we Know the name of the teacher but also; we Know, that we know it, and feel satisfied.

We mentioned that the human state is like a rosary with an especial amount of consciousness globes gathered together. After death if the deceased person couldn't find a way to self-realization, the rosary would be torn and the globes that each of them now have some important memories of the dead man would be freed and unified with the consciousness of the universe or God. This reality (which would be discussed later) means that the reincarnation won't happens always but only after you reached self-realization. As a matter of fact what we are working on is partly based on reaching a point, wherein, one can preserve his rosary of consciousness after death and would be able to pass after death and womb bardo consciously, to his/her next incarnation, or any other state he wants.

If the connector of the consciousness globes/strings be weak, it will be torn some day and each part of the internal knowledge the deceased had, would be scattered in the universe and mostly around earth (cause of gravity). These globes would be used for new packages and that's the reason; if you have not reached self-realization in your previous life, after deep meditation you will see scattered memories that are not exactly your own ones: one from a truck driver, one from a T.V operator, the other from a surgeon and etc.

If you had not reached self-realization in your last life you can never remember the whole top memories of one single person in your current life and declare that for example you were a doctor in your previous life. In 99.999% of cases we cannot remember all deep things experienced by one person. You'll find one or some memories of a baker lived in Tuscany, and the other may belonged to a poor pianist lived in Warsaw ….

Regarded to these discussion, the first thing that a student of spiritual path or rahro should work on, is to experience body-less consciousness by special exercises like those mentioned in references no.4,12,16 and 26(see writer's preface). Second, he/she should have a list of the most piercing and memorable memories. Third, do exercises for well-defining and finding your mind body, and fourth, do practices of unification with taba-tam and becoming sexless or null which would be talked in next session.

One of the questions every disciple asks here is: How can we become ensured that we have really made complete our ether and mind bodies? How can we become assured that it isn't a trick of our misleading and clever mind?!

This question has 3 answers: first; you will yourself know when you've done it. Second; a reliable sign is power. When A rahro/chela reaches self-realization and completes his/her bodies, becomes the king of his world and develops Will, and will rule on matters and fate(the reverse is not right). Third, meanwhile, every seeker should knows that there is not something 100%.

At the end of this chapter anther important thing should be mentioned. Scientifically it is believed that the "bipedal conscious creatures that lives on Earth and we call them human" are all a same Spices, and are named Homo Sapiens.

Actually, should know that there exists many, many different kinds of Humans on earth but they wear the same cloth of human form. This difference is significant to such an amount that some masters believe that the earth is the place for meeting of sentinel creatures from different parts of space. As you might noticed, except for rare opportunities that you may visit someone of your kind, or as some say; of your planet, almost all of the people around you are "Aline" proportional to you! They have different interests, aims, line of thinking, ideals, and definitions for good / bad. Something which is right in your point of view, might be wrong or even a sin in another one's.

So,.. you as the seeker should know this and be patient and pardoner and increase your acceptance.

Yes, it sounds that; different essences from different planets and solar systems, wore the cloth of human being form on earth and some are trying to walk in path of completion! But, how can one finds which way is right? the way of hemo-phili monsters of Mars, or the way of cold-hearted men from Uranus. The only compass that you and every human form have is "love and being conscientious". Each way you find more love, is toward higher state of consciousness. Don't forget this.

SHOW MUST GOES ON!

This stage of consciousness we call it earthy life, needs a large amount of energy, both physical and spiritual, to move and keep it's connection with 4th and higher dimension. This energy is provided by physical and mental interactions that happen between creatures, and of course human beings, living on earth.

- A snake curls around a frog and ate it semi-alive and some energy is exchanged between them.
- You embrace your lover tightly and inject your semen deep in her body, meanwhile a significant amount of spiritual and physical energy is transferred.
- A serial murderer cuts the head of a young man alive and the poor man struggles and think(even some seconds after his head is cut off) what was my sin?, why me…? and … Meanwhile a large amount of energy is released.
- A mother embraces her child who had been lost a few minutes ago, in the supermarket and another amount of energy is transposed….

What is important to the God or creator of this physical level is the energy, and the pupil should understand that; it is of no matter for the creator, how the energy is produced! If someone be at a low level of consciousness, close to the state of an animal, may for releasing the energy uses a device of torture but you as a creature at the higher level of consciousness may use hot kisses to your lover as a device of releasing energy.

So…, the most important thing that determines mechanism of energy transformation is consciousness level and you as human beings are the only creature that have the ability to choose to act like animals for energy transposition -by killing and hurting each other -or like angles- by making love and/or being companionate.

The earth is a classroom for souls they learn a lot here, and become a part of the god, or rarely a god in small scale. But this classroom like any other school needs energy to be open and old or lazy students that can't, or don't want transport energy are erased.

Now an important point; If only the transfer of energy is important, why should we do good works and be kind?(good works means the activities in which you don't hurt anyone) As the answer, it should be insisted that in mystic paths and theosophy the important point is, Not to make bounds. This means that a seeker/rahro should act in a way that no sticky bounds attach him to others. Most of the acts that are called bad are exactly the activities which create bounds on the doer. When someone hurts the other, though energy transference happens back and forth that satisfies the god of this level but, this creates a strong bound for retaliation which will halt spiritual progresses of the doer. It should be emphasized that some good works may also create sticky bounds, that is why when you are doing good works, you should do them with a "sense of not doing" it, and don't expect rewards.

Here a paragraph should be added; The God has different levels of demonstration, and though it can be considered as one, it has orders of hierarchy. In the first grade, what is of importance for the god that controls our physical world, is to keep the system(or as some called it correctly, matrix) on. Religions like Islam, Christian, Jewish call this manifestation of god "Gabriel", ancient Americans called it "The great eagle", ancient Gnostics of Persia called it "10th divine wisdom", and Indians call it "Kal". This manifestation of god never takes side for good or bad. It creates the killer tiger, and the Saigon's butcher or a devoted mother, with the same level of love and patience. Only those who want to play a different act from what they should, or reject their responsibility, or those whom don't try to increase their knowledge would be punished!

A seeker may find wedding parties or death ceremonies foolish. He may think becoming drunk or smoking too much or having sexual retaliations, or backbiting, is wrong. But he should not preach because for those who are out of the path, there are no other ways for energy exchange. They should enjoy alcohol…! The same as you, that enjoy mystic arts.

I KNOW THAT I KNOW

An animal or a planet never goes in search for god. They never create anything, on purpose. They never think and plan to build a house and if some of them make a nest or act something like that, it is preplanned. "They don't know that they know". We as human beings are an interesting experiment, created by the system! since we have a conscious thing (mind), inside another conscious thing (taba-tam/green tara). That's why, we know that we know and as a result, when we create something, immediately we ask ourselves, who created us?!

In last several millenniums, from the era of Hermes and even before him, masters described different definitions of the creator and when they passed away, normal people started to misuse it for their amusing purposes and created large misery and wars.

Of course any rahro/seeker should know that; the only reason such masters are permitted to write or tell something in the physical world is "the potential of their writings to be misused"!! which is inside their teachings.

The potentiality of these writings or trainings, for "being abused and become suitable for a source of interaction and energy exchange" is something necessary. So every pupil should know that all spiritual teachings are respectable and meanwhile should know that the great creator of this level, who uses the ignorance of human beings as a source for energy production, is not an awful thing. Since, he had put aside and improvised a secret by pass and gift for some knowledge-full creatures of himself;" path to self-realization". Every human being has the free will to go through this path, or be used as a simple creator and transferor of energy.

All symbols and writings about "objective knowledge"(meaning those knowledge that exists in universe – in contrary to subjective knowledge which man created and creates it) and spiritual paths, from seal of Solomon, Kabala, and Tarot, to Bible and Quran, all have the potential to be misinterpreted. This is not bad! Since ignorant people kill and/hurt each other during these misinterpretations and create great amount of energy, to keep the system on!

If you think this is cruel, first try to bring yourself up, and try to elate the mass knowledge and decrease ignorance of humanity. (Heh, though it will find its way again).

Anyhow, let's turn back to our discussion. If someone tries to kill a chicken, it will dies after a period of struggle(though don't know even why the chicken should make a struggle! But nature chooses those generations who fight for their lives). But, if someone or something tries to kill you, you know that you are dying.

Now, you as a student of mysticism should go one step farther. You should become able to observe yourself. In this state you should transfer your consciousness to the back of your head or even out of your body and see (observe) yourself when thinking, eating, walking, defecating,… and most importantly, having sex. For example, when eating a meal, you should be able to observe yourself and say 'it (your body) is eating. More details might be found in the books no. 13 and 26.

BASICS OF SPIRITUAL PATHS

A spiritual progress means travelling from lack of being conscious about "objective knowledge*', to a highest possible level of understanding of objective knowledge. We call the state of, ignorance to objective knowledge; darkness.

Here it should be insisted that God has two kind of demonstrations in our dualistic world; male and female or some may name it positive and negative.(A third force also exists that now we don't go through it. Only don't forget that we are 3rd force blind). Regarding this, loving another person or helping others or hurting others and etc, may have a male pattern or a female pattern. Male patterns are hot, dry, red and outrageous but female patterns are wet, cold, blue and deceiving. BOTH male and female patterns of thinking and acting, can be dark when are in their ignorant stage. So, the old belief that; male is positive and light and female is negative and dark is wrong.

- Objective knowledge means all the rules that the God created to arrange the universe; like the rule of 3(everything should accept one of 3 states of positive, negative or null), or the rule of gravity (every masses should flew toward the centre of the planet they belong to), or the rule of right hand of Fleming (when something curls counter-clockwise, an upward movement flews) and so on. On contrary, subjective knowledge refers to most of the scientific and non-scientific rules that human being created.

For going from darkness to light, there exist two paths on earth:

A; The positive or male path;(that was dominant, in human civilization in some periods). It sometimes, was called the path of white light, and civilizations and spiritual movements in ancient Egypt, pre-Islamic period of Persia, Tantric yoga in Tibet and India are examples of it. In this positive path the students of mystic arts were encouraged to study and gather a massive amount of spiritual knowledge up to the date and, to use daily life experiences as lessons by pondering on them. There was no objection for suppressing of sex power and in contrast, the strange energy of orgasm which is normally released into Ether, was used for consciousness separation. In male or solar path you make a journey deeper and deeper inside yourself, become separated of world hobbies to reach, or to form your real "I".

Meanwhile, for the people not interested in spiritualism, scientific and industrial progresses were promoted in male path period. That is why historically, great monuments were built in these periods of civilization.

B; The female or lunar or negative path (negative doesn't mean something bad! Remember the negativity of electron and positivity of proton. None of them are bad!), which is sometimes called the path of dark light.

Examples of this system for spiritual progress are all of the Abraham religions like, Judaism, Christianity and Islam. In these methods, celibacy and long fasting are promoted and sex and sexual energy are condemned. Instead pupils are encouraged for dancing exercises and recitation or Zikr, and the students are encouraged to travel outward and to experience unification with god even for a while.

In all of the long years of evolution of human consciousness, way to spirituality played back and forth between these two options. When the first mode was popular the clergymen claimed that their way is the way to light and the other is the way of darkness and satanic! After a millennium, when the first path began to putrefy, someone appeared with the essence of the second path and the followers of this second path screamed that their path is heavenly and the previous one was satanic and end nowhere but hell!

Many historical examples can be found for this; for example, in old African civilization, everyone interested in spiritual matters used male path. After many years, this path begin to be corrupted and misused by clergymen of that period. The Mousses appeared after this and correctly, suggested the female path. Later his followers claimed that the previous path was the path for terrestrial life and pleasures, so satanic, and their spiritual path is the path of light. In our era again a tendency is appearing to the male path(which its hallmark is attention toward sex energy).

As a matter of fact, the aim of both of these paths is guiding the student to self-realization and both are good and none is dark or satanic.

The ONLY bad and satanic thing for human is ignorance and consequently, prejudice toward a semi-completed knowledge.

Actually every rahro/seeker should experience and study both of these paths to be able to mix them at the end of his spiritual progress to reach singularity or sexless consciousness.

When you reach real self-realization, far from misleading and seductive mind, a continuous and reliable connection develops between you(as a "definable thing") and God(as an "unable to be defined" thing).*

- As a parenthetical sentence it should be mentioned that as a philosophical point of view, when human mind encounters something, it may accepts one of the following three states:

It might be definable, like everything we feel by our senses or able to describe, it might be indefinable, for example; angle, soul, love and so on, or it might be "unable to be defined" like God. God, because of its high dimensionality can never be defined by human mind. One which is in first state or world(like human), can never connect with the third state without using a medium in the 2nd state. Even if he makes a connection, would not be able to understand and analysis it without using an intercalary state. This state of middle is "imaginary or indefinable" world or state.

THE THEOREM OF KARMA AND RETRIBUTION FOR ACTION

During previous few millenniums a universal theorem has been disseminated between people by clergymen and some masters of female path. They said: "If you act bad or harm someone, you will receive bad results and something bad happens to you. So you should be peaceful and respectful to others, if you don't want to suffer". Even some Indians went further and believe that, if someone escapes from retribution in his/her current life, the karma will appear in the next life as chronic diseases and other painful sufferings.

Well….

Though everybody, and of course a seeker/ rahro should be peaceful and respectful to others but the reason is not for escaping retribution or karma.

Human beings have different options for consciousness or more precisely, focus (or attention) level. At the lowest level of consciousness- which he lived through in previous thousands year and still many are living in it, most of the things that happens to him is a result of accidents.

Imagine a box full of worms. They crawl on each other and the tail of one worm goes to the mouth of the other one and the waist of the other is crunched by the next one. If the tail of one worm goes to the mouth of the other is not because of the bad karma of the second or because the second one once has done the same. At low states of consciousness, and without focus, most of the things happen accidentally. But we as sensible creatures – or maybe for controlling others- connect these crazy random events to the karma of some other action, and sometimes more amusingly refer it to gods curst and rage, or on contrary His bless.

As a matter of fact when you live in a focus-less state, everything is busy and crowded. Today you may sprain your ankle and the other day a car may ran over your foot. These are not because of the bad behavior of you toward your friend you had three days ago, but simply because you are out of focus and busy-minded. If you be a good observer you'll see many people with very bad actions toward others, living in peace or many charlatan merchants and businessmen making more progresses every day, experiencing no karma.

Be sure that in their next life they won't experience a bad retribution also since they have not reached self realization and when not, there would be NO "next life" for them. After death they will dissolve and would be disseminated within mass knowledge of universe.

A next point should not be forgotten here. If you put your hand on fire, it would be burnt. This is cause and effect rule and should not be mistaken for karma. If you go late to your office repeatedly, you'll be fired. This and many others are examples of cause and effect rule. Again, if you keep yourself focused (or attendant) and conscious, you'll be free of cause and effect patterns.

We mentioned on the chapter for human creation that, at the time of synthesis of a human, a group of consciousness globes that once belonged to many other deceased creatures are gathered around and a new consciousness complex is made. At the time of this random collection, one receives some consciousness particles once belong to others and meanwhile is affected by the gravity of the celestial masses around him/her. These affections are called "fate".

Fate determines that, for example you should suffer dental carries more or knee osteoarthritis. Should you suffer the pain of your brothers' death or pain of bone cancer, or both? You'll marry a kind but unfaithful spouse or a disciplined and rigid, but faithful one.... So for finding the answer to this question; "why something bad or good happen to us?" the 3rd thing that should not be forgotten is the rule of fate. By keeping yourself focus and very conscious, even fate won't capture you.

For staying in focus and in heights of consciousness the first important thing is:" keep yourself away of interactions with others". This is the reason, why you should be good and compassionate to others. Being otherwise increases your challenges with others and decreases your focus and consciousness, which pushes you to lower levels of existence- world of accidents, bites and, cause and effect.

When you reach high focus level by practice and meditation and knowledge, you'll reach the power of "will". You decide what to happen and will become the king of your world. A little later you can rule the ether and may become a master. It should be reminded that: there are many good people whom believe that are masters, in fact they are teacher- and maybe even good teachers but not master.

A master not only should have knowledge, and be helpful, and kind to others, but also should be able to RULE ON ETHER.*

---

* There are 4 basic elements that are made from the formless matter. When you can rule on soil, water, air and fire, you have "will", and can rule on matter but for getting close to god one should have the power of interacting and commanding the 5th element(quintessence)or ether.

In this chapter we learned that all of us- whom reach this point of the book- are innocent and have no karma. If something bad happens to us is only because of our error in not keeping our focus and should be considered as a practice for progressing our concentration. So now, stand toward the sun and put your hand over your head~5-10 cm apart and palms toward each other. Imagine yourself (your consciousness) between the palms of your hands, then spell the word of power(Zin-uru) 3 times. You are sin-less now.

Put aside all the beliefs about karma and a God or a system that is sat somewhere and punishes you or gives you awards. You are innocent and if you make a mistake or hurt someone the God is not the thing that punishes you(you yourself decent your level of consciousness and focus to the state of accidents and diseases and inevitably some bad thing may happens to you).

So what is the role of God!? God radiates nothing but love. The same as you are alert about, and love parts of your body, God is conscious on everything. But, since we are in much lower dimension, if (as a disciple/rahro) want to be in continuous contact with god should make/prepare a something called soul body.

REINCARNATION; DOES IT HAPPENS ALWAYS?

If you be able to keep your rosary of consciousness away from being torn, at the time of death, then you may be able to reincarnate as another yourself after passing the Bardo of death and uterine life.

As mentioned earlier, what we call human, is a package of especial amount of consciousness threads or globes. Every person's pack of consciousness(which is alternatively called soul) is like air inside an empty bottle. When the bottle breaks, because of death, the air inside the bottle unifies with the surrounding air, and there would be no boundary to show you as yourself. In this case, which happens in most of the cases of death, the soul(consciousness + topic and unforgettable memories)would be dissolved in God.

At the time of the production of a new human soul, the "cast of human form" is filled randomly with proper consciousness globes which are taken from the dark sea of souls or as named in eckankar, ocean of love and mercy! This ocean or etheric space is something like a brew full of small consciousness globes and some larger poly-globes that belongs to semi-awake souls. In this space there are no significant borders so the data cannot be kept separate and at the time of taking a "cup" of this brew and creation of a new human soul, the resulted soul would have a combination of data/memories of different people. The only chance for reincarnation as a total soul (with memories of only one person) is to reach self-realization before death. So when we say., you should create a soul actually mean; you should well-define it.

In past centuries it has been made very familiar to many people the matter of reincarnation in earth or –reincarnation- in heaven or hell. Many people believe that they simply die and undoubtedly reincarnate in a good or wealthy state. Other, believe that if they die in a battle for god, they'll receive a new life in a heavenly state in earth or paradise. Still other believe that; though they are living in poverty, but after death they will reincarnate as a wealthy man or woman.

Though for ignorant people it might be better to think this way, but actually this is not always true. Reincarnation happens when you have reached self-realization in your last life. When you can not realize yourself and define your borders, immediately(or sometimes after a few days) after your last expiration and death, you will receive strong blowing and blasting shocks that will scatter you in the universe as primitive consciousness globes. There won't be a time left for you to complain! But, you may ask;"what about all the things I studied in religious books?" The future humans might have some part of you but not all. Your memories and knowledge are mixed with all the other souls immersed in the so called etheric space, or ocean of love and mercy. If you want to reincarnate as a super-star girl, or an Avatar, or a handsome boy, you should try to reach self-realization in this life time.

Now, with a delicate inspection you'll see that all the ancient schools and religions were right and each of them light up some part of the whole:

- If you reach self-realization in your life time, an Indian/Tibetan way will happens for you after death. You can reincarnate in a new body after the death bardo, and if you're father's sex organ attracts you you'll become a girl and vice versa. Here, the karma

of your previous life reaches importance- though a soul who has reached self-realization would have small negative or even positive karmas.
- If you couldn't reach self-realization in your current life time- which is true in most of the people living on earth, a Christian or Islamic way or pattern will happen to you. You would be scattered in universe and become unified with the god. This is the option that occurs for most of the human population, no matter they are Buddhist or Muslim or Christian. The only small difference with those ancient writing is this; there wouldn't be heaven or hell! Though everyone may experience heavenly or hell states as a karma reflection in his/her current life.

Now, See me carefully! you, as a seeker/rahro know that, reincarnation won't happen always, so there is no karmas of your previous lives for you. You are innocent and clean. If you experience some troubles in your current life, some are designed for your awakening, some are the back flew or the effect of your own activities in your current life, some are the result of interactions between planets' and stars' gravity, and finally some are the cash which you should pay for using these worlds attractions and beauties. There is no rage of god on you and you as a rahro should always remind yourself your chastity. And meanwhile keep your current life impeccable and errorless.

If an infant is born blind the reason in 99.99% of the cases is simply because of a defect in his/her human pack at the time of packaging of his/her human consciousness globes. At the time of production of human package or rosary or at the time of doubling some deficiencies may happen on the part which is supposed to live on earth. Of course these deficient states will give a new opportunity to the soul to gather new experiences and let them to be added to the universe or the ocean of consciousness at the time of death. However; in any case, the reason of congenital blindness is not that he/she made someone blind in his/her previous life.

The universe is full of conscious and powerful creatures. Some of them have body and some are body-less. Every student of mysticism should know that he should pay for everything that is made available to him by the powers which rule and set up this world, from the enjoy of breathing, to the ecstasy of sex. So, every rahro should have a frugal life without extravagance. This will make him unreachable to these powers and less tribulations would be experienced by him (the student). Meanwhile we should know that, the same as we use worlds facilities and creatures, we should not get angry or feel insulted, if we ourselves being used by others.

So, reincarnation, in a better or worse state after a death bardo(as Indian and Tibetan believe), or entering and beginning to live in heaven or hell(as Jews, Christians and Muslims say), happens in only one condition; When someone become able to "realize" him/herself before or at a very short time after death.

A good and persistent seeker/rahro, after few years of exercises will be able to keep his/her consciousness after death. The years of trainings should make him to be: A- Humble, B- nondependent, C- Frugal, D- not to live in a doing state, E- moderate in sex and wealth, and F- conscious about events on death bardo and dream state.

After these prerequisites he will reincarnate in a very better state(or as Abrahamian religions say; will enter heaven). For those at very high level of self-realization turning back to earth would be optional.

At the time of death of a normal person, who had received no ability for self-realization- like about 99.99% 0f Buddhists, Muslims, Christians, jews,…-, first they will see a brilliant light and meanwhile reunite with their taba-tam or green tara which makes them a good feeling like orgasm, then after a few minutes to hours they wake up with the terror made by severe shocks on the chest. It feels like someone strongly hit and strikes them on the chest wall. These devastating hits will continue until the package of the person's consciousness is destroyed and dissociated into its elemental globes that would be scattered in universal soup of human consciousness or by other means become unified with god (listen we don't say that this is bad. In contrary this option is also necessary). Memories of a simple clerk, a kind mother, a bad mother, a brutal murderer, an extremist, a nun, a prostitute… all, are mixed in this soup. In the soup everything should be in its appropriate level. If too much wars and brutality increases the ratio of meat in the soup, it will make the taste of it bad. Though, some amount of meat is necessary.

One of the points every pupil shouldn't forget is: ""the way of middle" for humanity and the rule of "never produce a bound", for himself, is mandatory."

As last point to this chapter, you should be known that there is also a negative way to self-realization. This happens rarely for very wicked and evil human beings. Large amount of brutality acts like a capsule for them at the time of death. These poor things will reincarnate in worst states….

DREAMS AND LUCID DREAMING

Our physical world as a whole and the human beings as a part, are under the influence/control of several, different known and unknown powers (the god of this level is the strongest of them). A usual man acts like a robot in the hand of these forces, and we can say that he is in a somnambulistic or waking-sleep state.

One of the best practices for getting the control in your hand is by getting the control of dreams or officially "setting up dreams". By these you'll gain power of dream control, which is the prelude to the control of your outside world.

Before starting this discussion it should be insisted that on contrary to most of the ancient mystic paths that respected the dreams so much, and named it;" the highest consciousness state of this time, possible for a human being" it should be insisted that Almost all of the dreams(in its routine way) are nonsense! Since, when you start to study them, the act of studying makes the dreams manipulated.

So, first of all you should learn to be an innocent bystander. And, second, you should try to create a dream body by writing the dreams that you've seen, after waking up, in the morning. Third and most important is, experiencing OBE. Out of body experience(OBE) and lucid dreaming are especial kind of dreaming wherein you are alert about yourself and/or your dream. This OBE is a very good preparatory practice for being alert about yourself in waking state.

It should be insisted that a state named "trance" is different with dream. This is a very important state of consciousness especially for pondering and contemplation, and actually is a kind of OBE.

Topics are as below:

- Before going to sleep make a will for seeing your hand in your dream. This is the best of "dream creation exercises".
- When you are going to sleep and at the very moment of diving into the world of dreams, try to resist for a few seconds. This will help you to keep and sustain your consciousness in dream state.
- You may concentrate on a bright letter like "A", located on your 3rd eye level.
- Watch the difference between outside, and dream, world. In outside world, events are continuous and one after another but in dream there is no time. For example your dream starts from a green beautiful meadow but you can't remember how you get here.
- Try to make your dream's sights and visions become sustained as much as possible.
- Try to go to travels during your dreams and check that the time zone of you and the place you traveled to, be logic and correlated, or else it is a common unimportant dream.
- The rule of "not-doing" should be extended to dream state also. This means, you should be an innocent by-stander and have insight that, these are dream sights which are playing. Any kind of interference will make the dream unreliable.
- To keep remembering yourself during daily life(to see yourself from outside of your body), will help the pupils to have" clear or lucid dream" or in other words, "conscious dreaming".

In our dream we cannot see ourselves. In the real world also we only see others and cannot see our eyes (that's why some Gnostics believed that the world is also a dream)! In more specialized language, we can't remember ourselves. For example this morning you saw your friend and you can remember your friend that you've seen, but you can't remember yourself when doing the act of seeing your friend.

A Pupil/rahro not only should try to see whole or a part (hands, legs, genitals or …) of his/her body in dream state, but should try to see and remember him/herself in awake, daily state. How?

By "will", or in better word " sustained wish".

Again it should be reminded that, you should invent suitable exercise for yourself. Exercises which are written in the related books on our reference list are good for beginning but you, after deep contemplation on them should find their essence and invent your own exercises. If unable to do it, this means you haven't found the essence yet. This advice is relevant for other chapters' exercises too.

ASTROLOGY AND HOROSCOPE

It has been mentioned that, after packaging of a group of consciousness globes or threads, a (temporary)human soul is created. This Soul or more correctly Minor soul (or as Christians say Father) is the mediator between material world (our physical body) and god or Holy Ghost. Respective to the kind of those globes and sometimes our affinities in after death Bardos, what we know as man or woman appears.

The whole of those processes are under the influence of cosmologic masses and astrologic forces.

Meanwhile, we should know that, this physical level needs a large amount of energy exchange for staying on work.

So, as a way to approach the whole universe, we consider it as; absolute Energy and Consciousness, in one end, and condensed matter with least vibration in the other side. There are many levels of existence between these two, from matter, back to absolute vibration. Between these universes there are always a continuous flew of creation and evolution made by transformation of energy to matter, or matter to energy.

Though the great universe has many more dimensions than the three that we can understand. And exactly that's why, we should consider it as a hologram(one in all and all in one), but hardly, one may consider different levels for macro-cosmos. The one below is one suggestion very close to reality, wherein, everything starts from God and after transformations turns back to God in a circular way:

Absolute God_ Absolute knowledge(Divine Wisdom)_ Creative wisdom(Gabriel or 10th reason)_ Ether_ 4 elements _World of Galaxies_ World of star_ World of planet and moon_ Absolute God

From each level to another, in most of the cases a mediator or transformative force should act. For example; from Absolute God to Divine wisdom, it is the "will" that acts. From Basic elements to galaxies it is the gravity force that acts…. In backward flow from planets and stars toward God the electro-magnetism and Large force acts as mediator.

From the state of planets- as representative of condensed matter, back to the pure energy, there is also one another mediator that should be mentioned:

The living organism, or the organic film living on earth.

As a matter of fact, the living organisms (and humans) are not the purpose of creation, but simply a mediator (or experience)in the current that facilitate transduction of matter, back to the vibration. The significance of human is very interesting as a new experience since he can transform the matter not only to EM but to a especial kind of energy named "impressions".

So, in contrary to some belief, the human is not the reason or ultimate of creation, BUT, it has the especial capacity to become the fruit of creation, by reaching self and God realization.

Because of these close relation of (living organisms and) human, with planets and stars, they have great effects on him, especially when human beings want to precipitate or settle down, and reduce the amount of interactions with others!

Imagine a glass of water with a spoon of sand in it. If you don't shake it, the sands will precipitate. This shaking is what the planets and stars do relative to semi-slept human beings, to never stop production of energy from matter. Whenever a group of human or a civilization reaches a stable and resting state these extra terrestrial forces do their job to deteriorate and revolute that stable state.

As mentioned before, between different organisms, human being is an interesting experiment. It is a duplicated creature, and this is the reason that he knows that he knows. That is why a human being has two parts. One, is its essence, and the other which progresses during his life time is "will" and personality.

Not only the planets, stars and galaxies affects on the package of human at its time of formation, but have effects on him or her, whole throughout the life.

Every human being is a package of consciousness states which is duplicated; one stays connected to the Holy ghost's context and is named "perfect Nature" or "Taba-tam" or essence and the other which creates flesh around itself, and is named human being. The cosmic masses influence on this second part only, and that is why you cannot predict exactly a human being's future by astrology.

Astrology is a complex science, and every student of mystic art should know at least, a little about it. You may find good and applied part of this knowledge in reference no.1.

As a seeker/rahro, though you have started the path but still you are in sleep-wakening state in most of the time. So, likewise everything happens to you in a preplanned manner (governed by cause and effect or busy minds around you or stars or/and…). But, by keeping yourself in an attended or present state, you'll be able to temper the calamities that will happen to you. For example; you are preplanned to attend a hospital for a major surgery like, open heart op. on date of yy/mm. By keeping yourself in a present state this can be changed to; going to the hospital for a small operation on a corn.

Now that we are talking about cosmos it is suitable to remind you that all of body-bound consciousness states, on earth, rotates counter-clock wise around the axis of earth. (In north hemisphere)this axis stretches to a star we call "polar star". Now that you know this, may use the polar star as a very good point of reference for consciousness projections. More details about consciousness exteriorization or projection will come later.

LAWS OF NUMBERS AND THE LAW OF OCTAVES

Some of the other mechanisms that shakes and move the world and force creatures to interact more and more with each other, are hidden in the law of octaves or law of seven, and laws of numbers. Discoverers of these laws were human beings of ancient life whom reached supreme conscious state. There are many people who work on these laws and try to find daily profits for them, but, the two profits of them for a student of mysticism is to show and prove him that, every ignorant human being is like a pre-programmed machine captivated under these laws. Meanwhile he become familiar with rules of creation.

In law of numbers each number has a power and meaning and every alphabet has a related counterpart in the column of numbers. Of theses some are of more importance; 4&8 are numbers of karmic settlement, 6 is the manifest of famine force, and 9 of the masculine force. More details in the ref. no 1.

Most of those people who experienced long lasting super conscious state, and Mr. Gurdjieff at top of them, believe that the universe is made by the interactions that occurs between 3 forces;

- Positive (doesn't mean good) or male or affirmative,

- Negative (don't mean bad) or famine or denial,
- Null or reconciler

This is called "the law of three".

In the law of seven, or law of octaves, the subject is about movement in time dimension. This law depicts that no state can be kept sedentary and continuous. You can not keep your happiness always or keep your mother alive always. The weather won't be suitable always, the sun will not shine for ever and .... It says that the same as an octave of for example major scale were in we have some semi-intervals(between mi& fa and si&do as an example in Do major scale), instead of full intervals, in the whole universe some breakages occur in every state that cause a new path of progress _most of the time toward sadness and suffering. Further this law points that, for keeping a state in its desired path one should enter a "shock" when a semitone wants to change the current direction(more details in ref. no. 20).

As mentioned before, what we see in the mythological books are some defective descriptions of these mysterious knowledge and/so, are not perfect.

MALE-FEMALE RELATIONSHIP

Why the opposite sex has deep impressions on us? Is it simply for survival of our generation? If this was the case we should go for it every other month or year, like other mammals.

As we have discussed in chapter for human creation, and as you will see practically in your deep meditations and contemplations; each human being is a unique collection of consciousness globes. At the very first moments of production, this consciousness collection has no sex. When we begin to create boundary around ourselves at the time of embryonic life, a polarization occurs and one part stays in the body and the other with opposite polarity stays body-less and acts as our mediator with other states of consciousness. This part, in every school of mysticism has different names, like; Taba-tam, green tara, soul, and…). Exactly this is why other animals are not interested about other worlds or studying and doing researches about god. And, meanwhile this part is the reason we are so interested in opposite sex subjects and affairs.

On earth we are always attracted by our opposite pole, because we see parts of our Taba-tam in some of the human beings living on earth. Since, each of us is unique, every human being may have a small part of that ideal counterpart that is living in other dimension. That is the reason why any male or female cannot find its ideal in his/her earthy partner.

After a period of 1-3 years in males and 2-5 years in females, they become frustrated of their present partner and feel a deep desire to find a new partner. Which is not a sin but a logic consequence of existence of a (minor) soul in human being. That's why we believe that, the public laws in every country should be changed in a way to make such experiences legal and without a sense of guilt for partners, and meanwhile preserve the stability of family for married males or females.

Let's back to the Taba-tam. This word -with a Persian basis- means; "something who has all the 4 basic essences in a well balanced state, in itself". Ancient Sufis and philosophers believed, every thing in our universe is made of 4 basic elements; air, fire, water and soil. Tibetans and Indians added a 5th; space. What ancients believed is not important here and if you are interested in them, may be referred to the reference books which are listed at writer's preface. What that is important is a process of doubling that happens in the case of human beings and makes a possibility for humans to create a bridge between known and unknown-able world. This event is exactly the reason that we are in a strange state of consciousness. We know that we know. We can create something and we know that we have done it. We make love with our partner and we feel and know that something strange is happening. We eat a delicious cake and not only our mouth become full of saliva and our body really enjoys of the act of eating, but we know that we are enjoying and something inside us also enjoys. All of these are because of the existence of a double. We are a super-computer inside another super-computer. Here is a very great point. The upper super-super computer can contacts us at any time and is conscious about us but the lower super computer can not connect the upper and is even ignorant about it in most of the cases.

One of the most important task for us in this world is to identify that super-super computer and create a middleman to keep your connection with it continuous. This is called "Real I".

If someone asks you; What was the color of the hairs of your teacher when you where in 1st grade of the school? First you may say; I can't remember. But, if you concentrate and/or contemplate on this question you gradually remember it. These memories that you thought are cleaned- and should be, since the brain doesn't have enough place for all of these data-are kept in your Taba-tam, or soul, or your picture in god's consciousness(many of mysticism schools have made different classifications of bodies- some 3 and others 4).

Actually, a vulgar male is not conscious about Taba-am. He is attracted to females only for sexual intercourse or unification and don't know why (since males has the misunderstanding of completeness). All the beautiful words that are transferred by him are only for deceiving and convincing (though the female part knows it also)!

About common, females the only basic terrestrial reason for attraction to opposite sex is a feeling of missing something and the need for finding a lost part to become complete.

As a student of spirituality you should know that the reason of sexual attraction and severe tendency for sexual unification is the separation which happened between you and your Taba-tam(or soul) at the time of your creation.

One of the most important things that a seeker/rahro should do during his/her trainings is to define and discover Taba-tam. It may appear to him as someone exactly the same of him or as a very beautiful angle with opposite sex. This second happens frequently, at the time of death and this is the reason many of human beings feel a sweet sense of unification and arousal at that very last moment.

PURPOSE OF CREATION

Many ancient religions believed that the purpose of creation was/is human being. But as you have seen in previous chapters, creation is a continuous flew and though the human beings are one of the best state of creation, they are not the aim. It should be mentioned that some human beings can, and may produce a great aim for themselves.

Before taking a look to the stream of creation it should be reminded that;

A: The energy of our universe has two extremes of existence: vibration and mass. There is also an omnipotent, omnipresent thing named consciousness which is out of our discussion now.

B: Physically, there exists 4 fundamental forces in universe.

- The gravity; that pushes the stream of creation from vibration to mass and tries to create more condensation.
- The electromagnetism; that turns back the mass to vibration.
- The large force(nuclear force or energy) works in stars to facilitate changing of mass to electromagnetism.
- And, the small force; it acts more at the level of planets and moons to change a little of mass to EM, wherein organic film - in some planets- also help for more mass to be changed to vibrations. (physicists believe that there is also a dark energy

or force that is unknown to them. Though, we think that what they refer is because of their incomplete and wrong knowledge about nature of gravity).

C: In the surface of the planets like earth, except for non significant cases like, small force, and rare earthquakes and volcanoes there is not a very good way to change the mass back to EM and close the circle. At this point the organic life comes in field and acts like a mediator. Actually the creation of creatures was only for changing a small part of mass and soil back to EM, by creating emotions and impressions. Of course human being, exceptionally has the ability to comes out of this automated circle, cause of especial –programmed or maybe accidental- structure he has.

D: As the very first step of creation, The Absolute, or Sugmad, or God or Ahura, creates absolute knowledge.

The absolute knowledge after many steps creates "the tenth knowledge" or Gabriel and this creates all of the galaxies, stars, planets and organisms we know.

Dear pupils should know that, this vicious and continuous cycle always repeats and repeats and though it has nothing to do with human beings, but we CAN make a purpose of it for ourselves. What is it?! "To come out of it and become a "small god".

Meanwhile, the consciousness globs or treads that are released after death of people and living creatures will make a large pot of globs that is called, collective consciousness. Improvement and progress of this brew also can be considered as another porpoise of creation.

As final part of this chapter, you should know that there is no Devil as pure darkness. God never created a devil a pure bad thing. The only devil or darkness, as some religions call it, is ignorance. To fight ignorant or semi-intelligent creatures, - whether in human form or as entities- it is not enough to have knowledge, you should have power also. By power or more correctly force(in mysticism force is a power that you've harnessed it and is accentuated behind a barrier to be released at its suitable time), you can keep them in a restricted region or area and give them enough time for their sublimation. And, If they are not sublime-able (like creatures other than human beings), they can act in their restricted zone as their instincts. That is why, every student of advanced mysticism should know a little or more about self-defense sports and also magic power applications.

Sometimes, people consider feminine manifestations of creative force as devil! This should be corrected and erased.

WHAT DO OLD RELIGIONS SAY?

We saw that, what we call "human or Adam and eve creation" is consisted of packaging of especial amount of consciousness globs, and then duplication of that knowledge package. One part which we know almost well is the one that has meat and blood or physical definitions, and other celestial part that is our connector with unknown world, is not well defined.

Meanwhile, we saw that the most important thing for the controller of our physical level- which is simply a creation of the great God- is mechanical and spiritual energy exchange, no matter with good or bad activity. BUT, the reason that we should seek for good activities is only for our own spiritual progress, since "bad" activities cause bounds and a deep need for retaliation in the oppressed one or vice verse.

Here a great question rise: What did the old religions talked about? They always stressed that we should act well and move on the delicate line of moralities, to make god happy of ourselves. Now we know that bad activities also make the system or nature or whatever you call it, happy, and the only benefit of not doing bad acts is for our own spiritual progress.

As a matter of fact, in ancient time, because of low level of social knowledge, there was a great need for combination of super-natural matters with moral fundamental laws. And, belief of an "only" compassionate and merciful god. In last few centuries, step by step we tried to write systematic protocols to protect the people's rights. In the 21th century not only there is no need to tell lies about the controller of the system, but if someone does, there would be many failure points for him. For example, why 39 millions of people died in 2nd war? Were they all guilty? All the people whom become blind in chicken pox and measles epidemics were bad guys? Why didn't God stop Columbus and Spanish aggressors or Islamic and Christian extremists from felonious acts? And...

One another point in old religions is the after death life. We mentioned this before, that; all religions are right but each see one view of the many options that exist.

Ancient religions believed: for having a happy and suffer-less life, you should always be a good man. But you see many good men around yourself with really pathetic life, And, many malicious people with acceptable lives. As a matter of fact:

For having a suffer-less life the only way is to consume nothing in earth! Since this is impossible so suffering is inevitable. Of course by staying in the path of frugality the suffering would be kept in its least level. Meanwhile being acceptable to sufferings consciously, and doing intentional reviewing of old sufferings accompanied by mocking them is a good exercise for students of mysticism to accentuate their non-physical bodies' boundaries.

AUTHORITY AND POWER VERSUS HUMILITY

In the path to self-realization there are lots to be learned, so a seeker/rahro should be humble and accepting, to learn every necessary thing. This will help him/her to decrease energy interaction and challenge with other conscious creatures- visible and invisible- that are scattered all around the earth.

This humility may create a pitfall for the student and make his protective aura become weakened or even perforated. This should be avoided since life energy will escape through this defect and will result in pupil's illness or distraction. A seeker should invent exercises for protection of his/her energy field, and don't let other creatures- human or non human- entre the shield. He/she should not create sympathy in others by begging and complaining.

The first step for keeping yourself safe and saving your energy, is to "become unreachable" for other conscious beings or states. This never means to hide yourself or go in caves or dark resorts, but before explaining this you should know one point:

Everything that we use on the earth or every act that remorse our conscience makes us to glaze for a while, in the darkness of the world.

So we will become visible for other conscious creatures. Becoming unreachable means to live without prodigality, don't telling lies, don't have a long duration of sleep, don't hurt other humans or creatures…. Of course, doing these should not put stress on you. Instead it should increase your energy and strength. If you feel a deep need to eat a hamburger, don't hesitate, as a matter of fact when you eat a cow's meat, this is great for the cow, since it is becoming a human(a little). Though, you also become a cow(a little). If you need sexual relationship, do it with love and never bother yourself with celibacy. When you stay in the path of mysticism constantly, someday your spiritual progress makes you to dislike meat or usual sexual relations. The reverse doesn't work(by celibacy or stopping meat digestion your spiritual level won't increase).

The second thing is; to act in a way, as if you are not the doer but your body is doing it- you are separate of your body whom is doing the activities automatically. And, you are only an observer. Consequently, you should never expect a reward or gratitude.

The third thing is; to have authority. Authority has two wings: Power and control.

Power is what some call "spiritual energy". And most of the people feel it unconsciously when receive appreciations or see a unique sightseeing, or making a fun of a friend or what they call as being in a good mood. Power or spiritual energy, in its very high level, is very necessary for a rahro, since in the very last moments of reaching self-realization and jumping to other states of consciousness, it is one of the very important things in need. As a matter of fact every human being knows unconsciously and feels that there is something out of this world and the reason that there are many different kinds of religions, ceremonies, drug abusers and rituals that believe that can connect their follower to those worlds is this.

Actually, a thick layer exists between our universe and other worlds and breaking this barrier without enough spiritual energy or power is like that drunk man whom wanted to break a thick wall with the knocks of his head.

There are 4 main ways for increasing your spiritual level of energy:

The first is by distributing it. When you bless or donate your energy to the world, a large amount of energy will come back to you. This can be done by helping others, protecting environmental ecosystem and…. Don't forget the first lesson; all of these should be done with a sense of "not doing", that means to do them without expecting to receive anything, even spiritual energy. The power or energy will come to you automatically.

The second way is by preventing waste of energy by stopping hurting others by bad talks, acts, or thoughts, and by controlling rage and lust.

The third way for increasing your power or spiritual energy is by turning on your own divine battery. This battery which is called "The pearl" or Kundalini or Libido in different cultures, and its worldly manifestation is the sexual affinity, would be discussed in another chapter.

The last way is by doing especial movements or using especial herbs and drugs. These are very complicated matter and should be done under supervision of a master.

About the second wing of authority, control, first it should be reminded that everybody is surrounded by an aura which is the result of interactions between his/her spiritual and materialistic parts(Indians have done large studies in this field and you may find more details in their related books). The outer layer of our aura acts as a defending fence for us against entities and dark human's thoughts. Control means that a seeker/rahro should make his/her fence strong and keep the aura clean.

This can be done by; especial kind of breathing exercises, or body statures like Tensegrity, yoga, and pranaya(more details in the book of Ram dass).

It should be insisted that, only using the power for simply visiting other worlds(the way that is frequent in users of psychedelic drugs) is useless, and most of the time all the experiments would be eliminated after turning back. A student should have enough knowledge meanwhile.

KUNDALINI A WAY TO POWER!?

To achieve a full state of self-realization and become a man of god or MOG, the pupil should become able of breaking the great barrier of, daily and routine perceptual input. Meanwhile he/she should became able of keeping his/her consciousness globs in a safe or definable package. All of these need a large amount of spiritual energy and authority. The authority as we talked before, has two wings; power and control.

There are many ways to gain spiritual energy and become charged, from outside sources. Some examples are; contemplation on beauty of nature, listening a beautiful music and/ or - mistakenly- borrowing and stealing it from others).

For last stages of self-realization those- low voltage- sources are useless. We have a great and much more powerful generator that can not only secure our energy for being elate and healthy, but also enables us to jump out of the boundaries of our "perceptual state of consciousness" and experience other states of consciousness before our death time arrives. This generator is placed in our genital organ and some doctrines call it kundalini.

There are many ways for stimulating your generator; from direct stimulation to mental awakening of it. Since in first decades of life the genital generator is automatically kept active by nature, spiritual progresses are faster in these years and on contrary in old ages, if you do not know how to keep it active, there would be nothing but a sedentary spiritual life. Ancient Tibetan spiritual men, and at their top Padmasambava wrote great note on this field and you may and should find them on the translations of Evans –Wants named "Tibetan yoga and secret doctrine".

Actually in every advanced spiritual practice the aim are to achieve two things: First; to connect the two spiral path of male and female, which ascends round the spinal column, at the point of third eye and turn the lamp on. And second; To bring the flow of energy to the central column or Sushumna voluntarily. This second also happens during sleep or death(significance of trance state in esoteric activities).

It should be severely advised that, a part of kundalini is necessary for normal life and you should not sublimate all of it.

MAN OF GOD (MOG)

When someone reaches self-realization and get the "power" for jumping out of this realm and live in other more delicate and diluted realms, consciously and on purpose, is called "man of God" or as an abbreviation MOG.

You should gather 3 items, each in very high level, to become a MOG; objective knowledge,(spiritual) Power, and Freedom of terrestrial hobbies.

Once, a great MOG said: There are four barriers for you to become a man of God.

First barrier is fear. Fear of unknown, and fear of losing social positions. A seeker should put every dependency away, never feel pity for his position, and exactly recognize world's games.

After putting away the fear completely you'll become powerful and exactly this will become your next barrier. For passing this 2nd barrier you should remind yourself that, the power you gained is not yours, but God's and you are only a channel for power transmission. When the power becomes under control and there would be no proud of having it, you'll reach a state of great peace.

Now, the 3rd barrier appears. Your peace state fills you with a sense of thorough satisfaction. At this phase the seeker/rahro thinks that everything is all right and he/she should do nothing. He forgets that this universal and thorough peace was not his aim. This is the 3rd barrier for continuing the path. For going out of this barrier the student should remind himself that this peace is not enough for jumping over the valley of death and that a long way is still left. He shouldn't forget that many things are left to be discovered, especially matters related to God-realization. (In all of the way till self-realization, a disciple learns and tries to go inside more and more, and separates him/herself of perceptually-made outer world. On contrary in God-realization he should come out and cheer up. He should turns back into the universe which is full of conscious creatures).

After overcoming the 3rd obstacle to becoming a MOG, the 4th and the most undefeatable one comes. Old age! Old age gives you a false self-confidence and meanwhile makes you to become lazy and to feel that the game is over. For pushing this last barrier back, you should begin from now, and by a prophylactic act, keep yourself young and healthy. Do regular exercises like yoga and dance. Keep your distance with alcohol and coffee, never overdose any food especially meat. Stay in the way of middle about matters like sexual relationships, business acts and job, money gathering and talking with others.

"Staying in the path of middle" is very important for one who is wishful for being a MOG, but, how may you find the path of middle?

The hall mark of the path of middle is non-turbulence. When you are in the path of middle in facing matters, everything goes soft and without making you tired and out of focus. The path of middle is different for every person. This is a very important point that was ignored by many ancient spiritual teachers. Consuming meat once a week may be the path of middle, about eating meat, for one person and might be once a month for another.

A rahro/seeker should internalize the knowledge, by reading books like those mentioned in preface, to become laden with the collective knowledge that has been found and gathered on earth during the last thousands years of civilized life.

He/she should find power by absorbing it from universe and learns how not to waste it, by keeping his halo capsule firm and clean.

He should reach Freedom by leaving his personal history, titles and dependency on fame and family (and finally his own body).

Only then a student of the path would be able to leave his body anytime he likes, on purpose. He can make actual and real consciousness travel, and would be able to die on purpose and meanwhile keep his consciousness during after death period or Bardos.

What is the benefit of this sustained high state of consciousness!?

When you're conscious all around the clock, not only you would be able to manage your terrestrial problems and use your good fortune properly in life time, but, after death would be able to keep and transfer your experiments to your next body. Imagine that you die on the age 90 as a great pianist and transfer your –internalized experiments to your next state of human form. You will become an indigo child with unbelievable abilities on early age.

PSYCHEDELIC DRUGS

As mentioned earlier we are bound by our perceptions and the way our mind interprets it. That is why we use meditation to experience what happens when these sensory inputs are stopped. This not only opens our mind to other interpretations but also will show that all of these pictures and even those after death are our mind's game. In rare cases, the student of mysticism is unable to experience this, and that's why psychedelic drugs come to field.

Most Psychedelic drugs, though change your sensory experiments, cause serious damages on nerve cells. These damages might be functional and sometimes irreversible.

Safe Psychedelic drugs which some of them were in use from ancient ages, Should be used only if, after at least 15 years of trainings about other states of consciousness and mystic arts.

Only if after that long duration of study and practice the seeker still didn't experienced a real "break through", under the supervision of a master or a good teacher he might use them once or twice but not more. Otherwise, it would be useless and in many cases harmful.

Of these drugs, those with least harmful effects are; Huma (a Persian name for a plant used in some Zarathustra rituals), Pyute, Psilocybin, and DMT. Though these drugs are really effective, but the seeker/rahro should reach realization, by knowledge and deep meditation. Trying to make a short cut by using these drugs in most of the times will cause retardation and break in discrimination between our daily world, which is our classroom, and other options.

Meanwhile, when one uses these drugs once, especially when early in the path, can rarely be able to reach that high state without using those drugs and there is a danger of addiction.

For more detailed descriptions the following booklet is useful; The Psychedelic experience by: Timothy Leary, Ralph metzner, Richard Alpert

EXERCISES FOR REACHING SELF-REALIZATION

It should be re-emphasized that a student of mysticism should walk the path on his/her own feet and should find suitable exercises for himself. The reason we don't concentrate ourselves on thousands of different exercises is this. Of course, some examples of these exercises are mentioned only to give you a concept of them.

How can you understand that the exercise is suitable for you?

Exercises that fits your system always creates in you a feeling of enjoy or satisfaction and even ecstasy.

As a matter of fact, most of the practices that the organizations and temples teach the followers and successors of a MOG or master, address their attendants to nowhere, and at very best, can teach them to live-and die- in a joyful state of ignorance.

Dear daughters and sons the only way to salvation —and self realization- is to pull the heels of your shoes and jump into the path bravely. By mimicking Buddha, Christ, Osho, Gurdjieff and other masters blindly, you earn nothing. You should find the essence and basis of their teachings and by contemplating and deeply thinking about them, find and even invent suitable exercises suitable for yourself.

Anyhow, the most important thing for reaching self-realization, is to have or create a deep and profound desire for beginning of spiritual path.(A)

The next important thing is to stay in the middle/moderate state- not bad not good(B).

As we mentioned, this universe that you are living in, needs energy exchange and though you are a student of mysticism, since you're using the properties and gifts of this level of consciousness, should attend in energy exchange too. But, you should first; always stay in the path of middle and second; do the energy exchange with a sense of" not doing it yourself". You should do everything without expecting any bonus since you have not done it! Something has done it through you and you acted only as a channel.

A disciple of mysticism should have a closed, well-defined and safe halo around himself(C). To do this you may study the books which are written on human aura or halo of energy, and don't forget that a successful seeker should not be like a pussy pigeon, as may many clergyman say, but should be more like a white lovely eagle.

We mentioned before that, "the show must go on" to make energy transfer and processing possible. Meanwhile, for keeping the people that are engaged in the game, ignorant, the system has designed some mechanisms. One of them is "internal talking". By this mechanism, everyone is kept busy even in restroom and sleeping state. Thoughts come by each other without stop, even when you sleep, after a short period of non-dreaming deep sleep(clear state), wherein you are charging your spiritual battery and refreshing yourself, the internal talking begins as dreams.

Hence, the next step to self-realization is to exercise; stopping the internal talking(D). One way to reach this, is by concentrating yourself on your inhale and exhale without disturbing its natural rhythm. This alsoshould be done with a sense of "not doer", or else, this act itself become an internal talk. One another way is by looking to a dot on a flat object and rotating the eyes counter-clockwise to come back on it after a circle.

Next mechanism of our trick-full mind for keeping the consciousness away from other realms, are sensory inputs. A great amount of sensory inputs from different receptors, encapsulate human's consciousness and won't let any new and different inputs. So the next step to self-realization is to stop them, from the simplest one (eye vision) by closing the eyes, to the hardest one- skin's pressure sense- by closing these receptors and omitting the gravity(E).

You may find many examples of these, on books written about meditation.

Periods of fasting, is also useful to slow sensory inputs from inner organs and slowing down the velocity of internal talking (F). How to do the fasting (liquids or everything) and its length depends on you. And, your body's abilities.

Don't forget that always should be alert of your activities (G). As mentioned before try to imagine(or in better words, visualize) that you are watching yourself in daily activities.

You should find the deep reason of each exercise. Only doing them the way ancient people said, is of very small benefit.

As it was mentioned before, though you are a rahro, and want to become a MOG, but now you are living in earth and fed from the breast of this level's god. You are using its space and creatures. The next thing that helps you in the path to become a MOG is; not to be lavish. Instead as said before, keep the path of middle in using the blessings. You should not squeeze the breast of world's god to get more milk/ possessions (H). Or else, this will make you accessible to other powers and stupid intelligent creatures living around you. This might end in physical and spiritual trauma.

Ancient Mexican MOGs used to say: "a student should be inaccessible". This doesn't mean to hide you from society, but means; not to expose yourself by asking a large amount or terrestrial things. Keeping yourself away from society, like what Tibetan once did or to condemn sex and male-female relation as priests and Muslims do, is not necessary in white-Light path, and only sometimes is prescribed in dark-Light(female) path. Only point is to use all the terrestrial blessings equinox and without prodigality.

A great mistake of some of the seekers is to preach for other people. They advise them stopping meat consumption, smoking, alcohol drinking, and sex affairs and so on. Don't forget; the reason that you can stop these is that you have a greater fun named the secret path. So, don't disturb others. If you don't want to play cards don't pull back other players or else, the guards of casino will hurt you! On the other hand, preaching so much may put you at the centre of attention which is harmful as mentioned before. Of course, you should be alert, and if you found a person, very interested in mysticism, try to help him/her.

After becoming expert in exercises on stopping sensory input, the next step is to exactly define that, where is your consciousness located (I). Many of us think that our very consciousness is located in our brain or somewhere between the eyes, but it is much more complicated.

First of all it should be said that the consciousness in mystery knowledge is made of two parts;

First part is you yourself, that acts like a detector or receiver and is made of body, emotion, And mind.

Second part, is your duplicate, or minor ghost, or Taba-tam, that transfers the received data to Holy or Major Ghost. It has been described that if your existence is with a so called male appearance, your duplicte would be a more with female parameters and vice versa.

You should try to unify these two the same as a man and woman makes love with each other (J).

Now let's do an experimental exercise. Find a comfortable calm place and sit or lean there back. Stop your sensory input by any kind of meditation you like. Now you can feel yourself in this state. You are in your mind, the place of your memories which differentiate you from others.

Now, leave the box of your memories from back of the head. You'll see that still something exists. A boundary less, hard to be defined thing, which still is you. This is the real you or "Am-ness". As it had been mentioned before, the small point of consciousness in spirit of universe that builds you is called the soul(or "I"). Now try to make an "I am" with your breath. When inhale go to "I" and when exhale go to "am". Now we put this practice, to later turn back on it.

Anyhow, more about sensory deprivation: There are many kinds of exercises for sensory deprivation. You may sit on a pillow in a quiet place and count your inhales and exhales or may lay down on a flat place and concentrate on your umbilicus or a place between your eyes(some called it the 3rd eye), and try to stop your internal talking(J). It is better to put a small stone on the place that you want to concentrate your attention. After stopping your internal talking try to find; where are you?, slightly and without distracting yourself.... You are(your existence is) placed at the place of your Concentration. Keep this in your mind and repeat the practice for a long time to find the essence.

As the next exercise, lay on a comfortable bed, the same as an old man experiencing his last minutes of life(K). Let the air of your lungs goes out softly, the same as a moribund...let it goes out completely.... For a dying man there would be no other order for inhalation but for you... !you'll see something finally orders for a new breath and you cannot hold your breath longer. Find the place of this re-breath commander. It is the place that your terrestrial "existence" and your higher picture in God's consciousness (as some named it "I") is placed.

After bounding your real I and your picture in God's body (your "I" and your "am") or, your male and female parts(your earth consciousness and your Taba-tam or green-tara), the next step is to transcend or displace this complex out of your body limit to learn how to stay without body(L). At this very moment, you will see that your consciousness has created your body's skin to make you well-defined and describable.

So, if you want to stay defined out of your body, you should learn to twist and twist, in a constant manner and very fast your unified complex(M). You may put your hands above your head, palms toward each other with a distance of ~ 15 cm, and imagine you are there between, and rotating like a torus. You may use sexual ecstasy of unification between your male and female part as a substitute for twisting. It depends on you.

If you're unable to move your consciousness out of your body, there are two, male and female, patterns that may help you. As we mentioned before both of these patterns are right and none are satanic! If you want to use female pattern(no matter if girl or boy), a very good suggestion is rotary dancing(N). Stand in an empty room, keep the palm of your right hand toward the sky and the palm of your left hand to earth. Now start to spin counter-clock wise. As you've read in basic physics, when magnetic field rotates counter-clock wise, a current happens upwardly that will mobilize your consciousness. In female pattern, repeating a word(mantra or ziekr) is advised(O). So you can repeat a syllabus or a word(preferably meaningless for you). For example, whole or a part of your name, or word like Huu, Heeyoo,...

If you want to use male pattern and have a male physical body, there are many kinds of practices. As an example...(this part is omitted by the order).

Now you should create a very fine capsule for your consciousness. Two things will help you. First; remembering of your periods of suffering, and second; doing all your activities consciously (R), like a computer that orders a robot to move. More details in books of master Gurdjieff.

(S) you'll see on reference books that it is very important to enable yourself to see and feel the vibrations of the ether or 5th element. These vibrations, force the other 4 basic elements(fire, air, water and earth) to get the various forms of matter on this physical plane. To do this, concentrate on your heart chakra or tiphareth(as mentioned in kabala) every day for a quarter to half an hour.

(T) we mentioned on previous chapters that everywhere is laden with consciousness. This is called "spirit". A very small part of the data in this vast majority belongs to you and is the creator or your mind and body. This is called "soul". So we have the familiar triangle of spirit-soul-body(mind)from above to below. Now if you want to go backward (from below or mind to soul) you need a mediator. Some call it Ether body. Actually every person during his/her living on earth creates such ether body. Create it During his responsibilities and internal talking. But, it would be disappeared shortly after destruction of body, since, we are not trained on protecting it during the shocks of death. That's why creation of ether body or more precisely well defining it, is one of the most important practices in spiritualism. The best practices for this, is Gurdjieff's one.

Don't forget that all the practices that you'll do on spiritual paths are only for preparation and declaration. You declare to the spirit of universe or as some call God, that; you are ready to be loaded by higher knowledge or powers and reach self-realization. But, the act of "giving" of these, are only done by his will and The God is the one who donates.

GOD-REALIZATION

PREFACE

Now let's begin the job we have come for!

Reaching (real) self-realization and be aware and conscious of reaching it, is almost inevitable if you study the first part of this book and all the books mentioned in preface, and do the exercises. And, keep yourself in the path.

In self-realization chapter we learned how to find the real "I" or essence of ourselves. Then it has been shown that a "something" exists in the universal named Holy ghost, which is definitely our creator. Finally, we saw that, there exists a connector between our materialistic state and the Holy ghost. This was named "heavenly pair" or Perfect nature, or Taba Tam. Its frank manifestation in us are; "conscience", and irresistible affinity toward stories about God, and of course, opposite sex. A disciple should find a way to unite these two and create a sexless thing named" I am". When "I am" is made, self-realization process is completed and the MOG becomes the real king of the world. Now this man of god has different options;

First, he/she may stay vividly on earth to the time of his/her death, and goes through the bardo of death consciously to turns back to earth as a clairvoyant and super conscious person.

Second, he may choose a "4 layered traveling" path, which is a kind of experiencing God realization state. In this path, the mystic whom is now a MOG, first will dissolve in God (but keeps his individuality) and all curtains between him and God is dropped. Then, he(whom is sexless) begins to see and experience God's patterns and definitions. At third step the fortunate MOG travels different levels of creation and visits higher states of pure reason. At 4th step of the travel, the MOG becomes a messenger of God and turns back to earth as a prophet.

Now, although wish you best progress. But;

Don't forget that all of the practitioners of spiritual paths are like corn seeds in a pot. Each section and type of exercise puts you all on fire and makes all of the corns to puff and jump but only one or two of these corns will jump out of the bowel (a metaphor of reaching self-realization) BY RANDOM.

WHAT IS GOD-REALIZATION

Why should we search God-realization?

During the previous part of this book we learned to do the mind cleaning exercises, stopping internal talk and go more and more inside by dissociating ourselves from world. And, saw that, Reaching self-realization happens apparently (to our 3-dimentional mind) by random. Meanwhile, there exists a time laps -of 10 to 15 years -depends on the globes of consciousness that you are made off(again by random). As a Rahro/student of the path of spiritualism, the only thing that you can do is; always keeping yourself in the path, until you reach real self-realization.

In self-realization you go to an inward journey. You try to omit sensory inputs and internal talking. In God-realization you are reborn again and turn back to the universe like a new blossom, but in a very higher state of consciousness. For god-realization these precursors are necessary;

- Opening(developing) of a higher knowledge receptor and transducer, called by some master, the "third eye".
- Unification with your Taba-tam or green tara which is called by some "internal marriage".
- Finding the real pattern and meaning of time and understanding, what is fourth dimension all about? The best description about

time is mentioned by Ouspensky in his book named tritium organon. By finding the meaning of time internally you'll see that the great options in your future, exist now. So the era where in you become a master of time exists know. Only you should find the way to go toward it straight forward.

- Reaching a deep and- as much as possible- close definition for God.
- God is a complete art work without any deficit and since you are made by That, there is no need to add anything to yourself. The only thing that you should do is to eliminate debris and superfluities. You should find the relation between the basic four elements with the 5TH element(quintessence). you should try to see the vibrations of these five elements.
- Though this may sounds strange to you, but you should be known that; everyone that you think about, or approaches you in all of your life time exists in your aura- or zone of consciousness. Or else, you'll never meet them or detect their existence. If you think about an alien from out of space or a serial murderer this means that they are in your aura and with you. So..., since you know Buddha, Christ, Moses, Mohammad, and other spiritual MOGs, this means that they are within you. You should only EVOKE them.

FINAL ADVISES AND MASTER'S LAST

- Try to keep your contact vivid with those who reached self- and/or god-realization.
- Choose some days of the week or month for fasting sections. Do the fasting the way possible for you, some are able to keep a full day of not eating and drinking, others only can keep a fasting for shorter, or only by fluids.
- As the time passes in your path you'll become disinterested to meat, alcohol and heavy smoking automatically. So, don't make yourself inconvenient. Whenever you felt a deep attraction toward a delicious Hamburger, go and try it. Don't forget this phrase:" for sure when you get close to Christ or Buddha consciousness state you'll put aside your bad habits like hurting other creatures or back bite and etc, but the reverse don't answer!(by don't hurting other creatures for reaching Master's consciousness)"
- Keep yourself always in the 9 fold path of Buddha or 10 commands of Mousse.
- Try to reduce your interactions with others. Be "responsible toward your activity and job in society and "forget your past"(never think that you are a great merchant, doctor, engineer

or so), and never do the "self-pity". These will help you to tolerate others cruelty, and keeping yourself humble.
- Stop wiseacre! You may have the temptation to advise a bad driver or an anxious man standing by you in the station, or complain your up-stair neighbor whom makes too much noise. But, there is no need for it most of the times.

Don't worry, someone who is at the same state of consciousness with him, will find him sooner or later and they will treat each other. For advising and wiseacre you should decrease your state of consciousness to the level of the person who is accepting it and this will make your defensive shield fragile, which actually may cause hurts or diseases.

Meanwhile, you should be always in search of some Remarkable men to transfer your knowledge to them. This is the only way for that your hand would become free to accept new gifts and knowledge. But first, you should become ensured that they are remarkable.

- If you accidentally found a real master(more precisely he chose you) that would be much better and will enhance your progress. But since there are thousands of people that call themselves(or their students call them) master, it's better for you to use the chosen books as your master until you reach the suitable clairvoyance to first meet your master in your lucid dreams then find it in physical world. Most of the masters you see in media and around the world are simply good, or very good, teachers, and not master.
- Except for periods of fasting and celibacy, enjoy your time in the manner of "not hurting others" and meanwhile try to share your happiness with the locals.
- The aim of the divine omnipresent consciousness of the universe is to teach you how elate your focus (projected consciousness). So, whenever your level of focus decreases you'll receive a shock

or punishment. Be conscious about them and when get one, try to deeply think about them to find the clue and return to path.
- Finally you'll find the rope and pull yourself out of the pool. Now that you have reached the safe shore, should throw the rope back to the pool to save proper souls. Don't forget that the only way to accept new packages of knowledge is to hand your knowledge to a new seeker.
- All of the students of different spiritual paths and systems are in the way to reach self-realization. As is mentioned, reaching self-realization happens by random, if someone reaches it this never means that God loved him/her more than the other students, or he was a better practitioner. Never become proud of any kind of spiritual progress.
- Mark and well define some unique event of your life which you where at its centre and from now on, on every unique or lovely events, try to visualize yourself and the event from above.
- Don't make too much noise or wiseacre. Don't build cults, temples and churches!
- Never try to convince others by phenomenon experienced by you. The most astounding ones would prove nothing to those who are not convinced already. Don't forget the 4 rules of alchemies; know, dare, will, silence(Levis).
- During the period that you are living in your physical body, not only there would be a need for food, Oxygen and water to keep you alive, there is a continuous need for impressions. Your body and soul need deep impressions, which can be absorbed by; deep thinking on music, and nature's beauty, watching emotional films, remorse of conscience, and spiritual matters and so on. If you don't try to accept impressions from these patterns, "unexpected events" will come to you to create deep impressions. So this should be kept in the mind of each pupil.
- After all of these years and practices you should be able to see and feel without your body. Only then you can take your

consciousness all through the very complicated and wired bardo of death and reach a new human body. If death approaches you, before reaching this very important state of self-realization it would be better to give up everything and let your consciousness be dissociated, and dissolve in God's universal consciousness- the same as vulgar people. Or else, danger of being incarnated in lower states of creation, like a dog or a stone state for very long years, exists.

CPSIA information can be obtained
at www.ICGtesting.com
Printed in the USA
BVHW032206300619
552359BV00005B/121/P